MY FIRST Puppy

By Alyssa Satin Capucilli

Photographs by Jill Wachter

Ready-to-Read

Simon Spotlight

New York   London   Toronto   Sydney   New Delhi

For Maya Madelyn and her beloved Charlie!

—A. S. C.

Dedicated to all the love that pets and their

young caretakers share. All the smiles they

bring light up the world.

—J. W.

SIMON SPOTLIGHT
An imprint of Simon & Schuster Children's Publishing Division
1230 Avenue of the Americas, New York, New York 10020
This Simon Spotlight edition December 2019
Text copyright © 2019 by Alyssa Satin Capucilli
Photographs and illustrations © 2019 by Simon & Schuster, Inc.
For information about special discounts for bulk purchases, please contact Simon & Schuster Special Sales at
1-866-506-1949 or business@simonandschuster.com.
Manufactured in the United States of America 1019 LAK
2 4 6 8 10 9 7 5 3 1
Library of Congress Cataloging-in-Publication Data
Names: Capucilli, Alyssa Satin, 1957- author. | Wachter, Jill, photographer.
Title: My first puppy / by Alyssa Satin Capucilli ; photographs by Jill Wachter.
Description: First edition. | New York : Simon Spotlight, 2019. | Series: My first ; book 8 | Audience: Ages 3 - 5 |
Audience: Grades K-1 | Summary: "Find out what it is like to get a new puppy in this beginning reader by Biscuit
creator Alyssa Satin Capucilli. What will it be like? You will teach your puppy to sit, take it on walks, feed it, pick
up after it, learn to pet it gently, and most of all, love it very much! Young readers will love seeing photographs of
kids their age take care of puppies in this adorable introduction to pet ownership that includes a special section
in the back with even more information about having a pet!"– Provided by publisher.
Identifiers: LCCN 2019029162 | ISBN 9781534453807 (hc) | ISBN 9781534453791 (pbk)
ISBN 9781534453814 (ebook)
Subjects: LCSH: Puppies–Juvenile literature.
Classification: LCC SF427 .C353 2019 | DDC 636.7/07–dc23
LC record available at https://lccn.loc.gov/2019029162

I am getting a new puppy!

Today is the day.

Her bed and food are ready.

I cannot wait to play!

My new puppy
sniffs my hand.
That is how he says hello!

Then we put his collar on.
Off we go!

My puppy must learn to walk on a leash.

I stop and wait a bit.

I teach her to come
and stay.

I can teach her to sit.

I can give my puppy water.

I fill his food dish, too.

I brush and pet her gently.

There is so much I can do!

Uh-oh! My puppy went
potty inside!
We clean it up right away.

He will learn to go outside
if we teach him every day.

It is fun to play fetch.
My puppy likes
her ball.

Playing with my puppy
is the most fun of all.

Puppies love to chew.

I put my things away.

I want to keep
my puppy safe
each and every day.

My puppy wags his tail.

He is happy as can be.

Having a pet feels great!

My puppy is a friend to me.

Your New Pet!

Are you ready to care for a new pet?

Let's learn about a new puppy and its needs!

Ask a grown-up to help you read more about

how to care for your special friend.

Welcome Home!

It's time to welcome your new puppy home!

1 A Bed or Crate

Be sure your puppy has a clean, quiet, and comfortable place to sleep. Your pet may like a soft bed or a cozy crate.

2 Things to Cuddle

A cuddly blanket or toy will help your puppy feel at home.

Getting to Know You!

1 Sense of Smell

Sniff! Sniff! Did you know that puppies use their sense of smell to get to know you? Gently let your puppy sniff the back of your hand. Use a soft voice, too!

2 Choose a Name

Soon your puppy will get to know his or her own name. What name will you choose for your new pet? Sunny? Charlie? Spot? Luna?
Be sure to use your imagination!

Learning Together!

1 Walking on a Leash

You can choose a colorful leash and a collar that fits your puppy well. Soon your puppy will learn to walk by your side.

2 Sit, Stay, and More!

In time you can teach your puppy to come, sit, and stay. You can also teach him or her to roll over, fetch, and shake your hand. Be patient! Remember, your puppy is learning so many new things!

3 Going Outside

Your puppy will learn to go to the bathroom outside.
Be sure to reward him or her with a treat.
Good job!

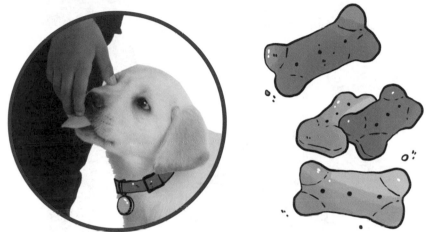

4 Being Patient

Having a puppy is a lot of fun, but it takes time and
patience and practice! As you learn how to keep
your puppy happy and safe, your puppy will learn
how to be well-behaved too!

A Healthy Pet

1 Food and Water

Fresh food, clean water, and exercise will help your puppy grow strong.

2 Checkups

Did you know a veterinarian is a doctor for animals? A checkup with the veterinarian will make sure your puppy is healthy and ready to make new friends.

3 A Wagging Tail

Dogs can't talk, but they can let us know how they are feeling. A wagging tail can mean that your puppy is happy!

4 Always Be Gentle

It is always important to pet your puppy gently on the back, not the face.
Never pet a dog you do not know without asking its owner first.

5 Stay Safe

You can help keep your puppy safe. Be sure to always clean up any small things your puppy might nibble on so he or she doesn't swallow them by mistake.

Your New Friend!

Some dogs are big, some are small.
Some are old and some are very young! No matter
which type of dog—or other animal—you choose as a pet,
with lots of love and care he or she is sure to become your
best friend!

**Is your family thinking of getting a new pet?
Consider adopting a pet from a local animal shelter.
Many pets need homes and a best friend like you!**